Rowland Joseph (left), horseman and market gardener, with his brother Edward, 1930s

In memory of Nick Bellorini

RIDGE & FURROW

Voices from the Winter Fields

Neil Sentance

Neil Sentance

LITTLE TOLLER

Contents

Old field names, as recorded in the Goosegate Farm inventory
(April 1923):

First Salt Moor
Bean stubbles now growing wheat
Twice ploughed
Sown and prepared,
Harrowings,
Seed wheat

Corner Salt Moor
Summer fallow now growing wheat
Orders, rent and rates
Drilled and prepared,
Harrowed,
Seed wheat

Far Salt Moor
One year's seeds, mown, now growing oats
Ploughed
Drilled,
Harrowings,
Seed oats

The Meadow
Grass mown
Twice chain harrowed, Spring

Peaseland
Growing beans on oats

Sand Dyke
Growing wheat on mangolds

Middle Lassum
Grass mown
Twice chain harrowed, Spring

Artificial manures applied according to the Lincolnshire custom

1985

Hope Gardens

Frank forked another small load onto the bonfire. A stook of paper coiled inwards and hissed. Smoke furled into the air, and drifted through the last frayed heart-shaped leaves of next-door's lime tree. Frank took an involuntary step back as the heat scorched his eyebrows and his combed-flat hair. The fire wheezed. Some ashy shards caught on the pocket of his worsted cardigan. He brushed them off, rubbed his aching wrists and then adjusted his tie, now a quarter-inch skew-whiff. He lifted his head and shielded his eyes with his hand. The weak sun emerged from behind a cloudbank and then was washed out again, overlaid by a shimmer of flocking knots, wintering shorebirds that veered back and forth in a pulmonary rhythm and then off towards the salt marshes at Fishtoft and the Freiston Shore pillboxes.

Frank straightened his long back and looked round his small garden. The privet didn't need a trim, but he'd probably do it anyway. A pale shadow played on the newly creosoted fence panel, the hazy outlines of two fat pigeons sitting on the garage roof like punctured blimps. They'd be at the vegetable patch soon, but it had only doughy potatoes left in it. The lawn was short and neat, deep-green and mossless, and would have pleased his pals at the Bowls Club. The copper beech hedge in the shaded corner was still thick and boxy. Its fallen leaves carpeted the ground, taking so long to decay that Frank had to rake them up every day at this time of year. His mother once told him that as a child she would gather the leaves for stuffing mattresses, but to Frank they were neither use nor ornament. He'd go in, he thought, in a minute – it was a cold day, late in a wintery year, and the world seemed like the inside of an upturned mixing bowl. He poked at the bonfire, but the heap of old files and cheap yellow papers had burnt up quickly. Years of paid-up bills, newspaper cuttings, his late wife's shopping lists, birthday cards, army communications, letters from hospitals, the long correspondence – with a brief blaze and gone.

Frank carefully placed the pitchfork in the turf and shook the dirt off the corded veins of his hands. He walked over to the potato patch. Morning toadstools exploded underfoot in a puff of dewy spores. He bent down, one hand on his knee for support; with the other he clasped a handful of earth. The soil had been raked and smoothed and a ridge of loam curved down to the end of the patch. He couldn't recall working it. Truth is, he'd rather let it go since his wife had died. He remembered his father, even near the end, carrying on digging, hoeing, scraping, planting, twisted with pain but still claiming the earth as his own. Until, of course, it claimed him.

Frank went back in, to the small kitchen little changed since he and Lottie had come here in 1938. He'd been a young man then, newly married and moving up in the grocery trade. He had served his apprenticeship at a certain Alderman Roberts' store in his home town – he remembered the old man's daughter Margaret, even then all elbows and avidity, but it was better to say little, now that she had risen so far in the world. Soon he had progressed to Home and

Colonial Stores and then to manage the Lipton's grocery shop in the old fenland town of Boston, where the River Witham sluices out of the flatlands and into the Wash. He had met Lottie, a sales assistant in Keighley's linen and drapery, and five years older than him, at her sister Midd's boarding house, where Frank had his digs on first coming to the Fens. Tender words at the dinner table led to Sundays stepping out and after a year or so they had married in the great parish church, St Botolph's, with little ceremony but with buoyant hearts. In their wedding portrait there may have been a tentative inch of daylight between them, but never thereafter. Frank's father had died only the day before, nursed to the end by Frank's mother and stay-home sisters, but Frank was all purpose and go-ahead now, a staff working under him, his salary a princely £5 a week, the world full of vernal promise. The newlyweds soon had £20 down on a £100 mortgage for a new-built semi in Hope Gardens.

This was all before the war. Frank went to boil the kettle on the stove and started when the gas ring popped as he lit it. He still had the routine of making a pot of weak tea for two. He reached for the biscuit tin. His back was sore. He could see through the window the pigeons from the garage roof, now pecking at the cracks in the path outside, white-manuring as they doddered along. He brushed the crumbs from the countertop and cast them outside for the pigeons. Tired out, he decided to go and have a lie down, 'up the wooden hill' as his father used to say. Passing through the hall, he righted the retirement barometer that always hung a little off-kilter, its needle permanently skewering the curlicue C of 'Change'. He climbed the stairway, hand tight on the chamfered rail, not glancing at the old photographs in thin frames hanging on the wall. But once on the bed, sleep wouldn't come. He closed the curtains, but a pool of dim-watt light from the landing lapped at the candlewick.

Motes of dust drifted across the room and settled on a pot plant. Aspidistra? He couldn't remember – Lottie would know. He could hear the quarter-hour Westminster chimes from the mantle clock downstairs. Outside, there was small rain now, scuttering on the windowpane. He felt flushed, a little feverish, and empty. He stared at the wall but the Bakelite lightswitch seemed to swell and then shrink before his eyes. He turned away as the floral pattern on the curtains swirled and eddied. His legs twitched in the maddening spasms that he had had since a child. He cursed, mildly, under his breath, and looked at his gold watch. He knew he had to get up.

Downstairs again and restless, he decided to take out the car. For once remembering to pull out the choke, he backed out of the tiny wooden garage with a grimace as he glanced back over his shoulder. He was a poor driver – he had only gained his licence through riding motorbikes in the war, and was ill at ease behind the wheel. His first car he had smashed up on the Fosse Way in Leicester and ever since he had peered over the dashboard with faint terror. Clanking the gears into first, the engine sputtering, he noticed the gaps in the rotten boards at the bottom of the garage door. He would have to ask his nephew to fix them up.

He drove out, crossing the Maud Foster Drain and past the Pilgrim Hospital, where he had of late spent so long with Lottie, holding her shrunken hands in his own. He was soon into the Fens, flat as an empty diary page, long gridded fields looking like a sodden electrical diagram. He made for the coast road, towards Skegness, over the arrowing Hobhole Drain, and on through Old Leake and Wrangle. Closer to the Wash, church steeples like the mainmasts of landlocked ships seemed pencil-sketched on the horizon. The light was now miry, the car headlamps smudging the nearing darkness. The windscreen wipers swiped on intermittent.

At Friskney he turned off and went slowly down the Eau
Dike Road and by the Barley Mow pub, where his eldest
sister Daisy had been sent to live with a childless aunt and
uncle, all now long gone. Frank drove down the Old Fen
Bank and onto the roddon, the dried raised bed of a one-
time stream. Trees were few, only the weave of carrs of alder,
willow and birch at corners of field rows of vegetables and
rapeseed. Eerie brick farmhouses were built on the silt ridges,
seemingly long abandoned and yet with old sheets flapping
on the washing lines, or thin brindled chimneys of outhouses
faintly smoking. Sometimes there was a lone pony or donkey
tied to a gatepost, motionless, head down, withstanding all.
The reclaimed land here was still under the sea's charter.

Frank neared a café he had known on the Wainfleet road,
but didn't stop – these days he found he struggled for words,
even in simple transactions. In any case, he didn't like to eat
out alone. He stopped the car in a lay-by. He remembered
coming out here with Lottie, sometimes along with his sister
May and her husband Bob. One high-sun afternoon before the
war they had laid their picnic blankets on tussocky mounds,
hoping for an easy half-hour nap, but were soon assailed by
yellow meadow ants crawling out like shattered battalions,
the men dropping their lit cigarettes on top of them. Now
he stared out over dark braided streams oozing through the
fields, and the lapwings nodding on the ploughlands. A slack-
winged rook lifted out of a scrap of hedge, all rag and bone.
A landward breeze was rising, direct from the Urals as they
say around here. Frank felt he could see the wind, like time,
coming towards him. He closed his eyes.

The returning dream. Frank is walking across a blank
bare field in early morning in winter. The clay heaps under
his feet, the furrows lengthening all the way to the stripped
hedgerows beyond. A hare makes to scamper across his path,
but sees him, coils and bolts the other way, gone in a breath.

Then he sees his father, tall, thin and stooped, standing at the field edge, with a horse and dray, loaded with sacks of potatoes. The nag is panting heavily into a hessian nose-bag; the dray's wheels are slowing sinking into the clag. His father's round face is expressionless, his hand scratching the thinning bran-like hair on the top of his head. His father starts to move off, his left leg dragging, legacy of a horse-kicking when he was chauffeur at the Cafferata plasterworks. He'll be off to look over his wild Irish ponies that his wife will break by hitching to the dray. Frank hears the metrical creak of the cart as it moves along the rut. He starts to follow but then stops. Two gunshots sound, close together. A loose column of black crows rises over a wood. The dream has shifted. His father is now outside a pub, back in town, in Wide Westgate, the Blue Ram. He's standing underneath the red-brick archway, his arms outstretched above him, so it seems like he's unsteadily holding up its span. He's drunk a bellyful. It's after closing time and he's soon back in the dray, the weight of sleep upon him, the horse knowing the way home. He's been drinking heavily these last years. And he's been horse-trading again, his cash stowed on his person, sewed into his weskit, never trusting the banks with his money, and, kaylied, he's bought another knackered horse. Frank knows he'll sober up in the morning and tell him to take it to the slaughter yard: 'And make sure it don't fall on you on the way!' His father draws away. Frank wants to call out to him, but doesn't, and is left looking after, mud up to his ankles.

Frank woke with pain in his leg. He gasped and bent to rub it. One of his 'war wounds'. Five years and seven months, a bitter service, gunner in the Royal Artillery. In April 1945 he'd been part of the liberating army at Bergen-Belsen concentration camp in the heathlands and flat moraines of northern Germany. He could smell it on the approach, the mephitic air: some 13,000 corpses unburied outside the barbed wire of the camp, dunes of abandoned humanity dumped under groves of budding trees. He had spent weeks there, in a daze, in suppressed horror, tending the sick and dying, burying the untold dead, doing what he could. He never got used to the clamouring of wasted, twitching hands, beseeching and hope-bled. Death encircled. His best pal was killed pulling the chain on a booby-trapped WC. Boarding the boat back to England at last, Frank collapsed with peritonitis, and nearly died in a French hospital.

While recuperating, a German prisoner had painted his portrait – Frank in uniform is still gentle, kind, quiet, particular and smart, but his eyes are anguished and his brow deep-lined. He knew he looked beside himself. To while away the hours, they played chess on a small kitbag board, although the white king was missing, and the German POW played a cannier game. Back in Boston, and to Lipton's, he'd tried to pick up the old life, but the war had ruined his health and his nerves were splintered. He and Lottie were now too old to have the family they had always wanted. Some years later he had developed TB, and he spent the best part of two years in London Road hospital hooked up to a spinal tap.

Frank started the car and turned on the headlights. He drove home thinking of the poor state he'd been in when he eventually got home from hospital. He had had to wear a full-torso leather corset, his spine sintered stiff and his posture so rigid it had made him feel older than rolled stones. He had become depressed, his thoughts taking serially to the air, a disorder of the mind where associations come undone. He had become convinced it was all divine retribution for not visiting his parents during their final illnesses – he was haunted by his sister's description of how they had had to drip water from a goose quill into their father's arid mouth as he lay gasping on his deathbed. But Lottie had comforted and supported him and he had found solace in hard work, all hours, most days, weekends included. He only retired when the shop was closed down in the early 1980s. He took up crown green bowls, like other dapper men of his generation, finding its easy rhythms and slow skill a distraction from the aching.

It was dark when he got home. He stood at the garage door for a moment. The Boston Stump, the soaring lanthorn tower of St Botolph's, was lit up like a sea mark. He couldn't smell the sea though, only the trace of something like the inside of old straw bales that reminded him of the Lipton's shop. In fifty years of being here, he'd never been up the tower. Lottie had been scared of heights, but he would have liked to look over the sweep of the Wash and the slow gradation, the dissolution, to waterlands, where the sea made its negotiations with the shore. And to gulp the high, pure air into his punished lungs in the unearthly realm of the summer swifts and falcons. The shrubs near the bay window rustled. Next door's bare maple swayed. The wind would pick up and scour the east country overnight. The night was thickening. Frank caught his breath. The street lamp reflected in the ribbed glass of his front door as he put the key in the lock and entered the empty house. As he unbuttoned his coat in front of the hall mirror, Frank thought: *I am a man made of smoke.*

A few weeks later he went into his garage and checked the rotten plank in the door that his nephew had just mended. He fixed a hose to the car's exhaust pipe and through the quarter light window, sat in the driver's seat and started the engine. He revved the accelerator, once or twice, and turned away the rear-view mirror. Then he waited for the upwelling of flue gases, and release.

1963
Dreams of the Old West

The television screen flurries grey as the set warms up, with its familiar faint resinous odour and low hiss. It's a Sunday in early February, past teatime and now into the slow slide towards the working week. Later that night, Cliff Michelmore, the unruffled host of BBC's *Tonight* programme, will report on 'The Big Freeze', one of Britain's coldest winters of the twentieth century, thick snow covering the country from Cornwall to Scotland since Boxing Day. That same cloaking snow is now hauled over North End farm like a silent home-grown ocean, no hint of brick-red earth beneath. It drifts over the gridded pastures and arable acres, high-yield plains and hollow spinneys, over the black beck and its broken ice sheets, the hispid hedgerows, the dead ponds and the solid pumps, over the metalled road and the drover tracks, the low fields and the heath, over the dairy shed and the pens of huddled cattle and the high fences, into the mouths of old barns stuffed with frozen straw and up to the cream windowsills to mass behind the back door of the farmhouse.

My mother, just turned seventeen, has soaked in a lukewarm bath and her dark hair is wrapped in a towel.

She is now curled up on the settee, comfortable in her black sweater and turn-up jeans, looking, if only she knew it, like a French film starlet. She hears her father come into the kitchen from the stack yard, resting his shovel by the back door, ready to dig his way out in the morning. As he stuffs newspaper into his wet boots and shakes a frosting off his flat cap, she notices through the dining room hatchway how much he resembles the late Hollywood actor Ward Bond, another thick-set and square-shouldered hard-driver. My mother is waiting to watch the star in his role as Major Seth Adams in TV's *Wagon Train* – for she, along with her sisters, loves westerns. As her father goes upstairs to draw his bath, the house is otherwise unusually quiet. Her mother is still in hospital in Nottingham, after the birth of her fifth daughter last Wednesday. Her sisters are all preparing for school tomorrow or are at the chores – Mum has laboured long today, in the house and in the yard, as on any day, and feels no guilt in her hard-earned rest. Granny Holmes, the dinner cooked, the washing up done, left an hour ago – once again she had made a silk purse out of a sow's ear, a kingly meal out of the orts and scrag-ends, a template my mother will make her own. A small table lamp gives the weak light. It's snowing again outside, but only a languid flecking and Mum has a cherished moment of peace to herself.

She has a plate of dripping on toast resting on the arm of the settee. She has risked two bars on the electric fire. She'd prefer *Bonanza* or *Rawhide* on the TV, but *Wagon Train* has grizzly old Ward Bond and it's the solitude of the front room in a close-packed house that is the big draw. This evening Mum can indulge her passion for the Old West on her own. Years before, Grandad Holmes had flamed this delight for western tales – he'd be there in his kitchen rocker, his hands cradled on his paunch, as Mum would choose from the dresser crammed with cheap volumes of Zane Grey, Jack Schaeffer and Owen Wister. From then on, the country she played in as a child became the Great Plains and Monument Valley, the chalky Lincoln mesa threaded with muddy gulches, the tinkling River Witham her proxy white-water Rio Grande. The Loveden Hill wapentake became the arroyos of the Arizona Territory, the GNER line was the Pacific Railroad, and on the wide-open pasturelands below ranged steers and beeves, and even fanciful bison, haunting the badlands. To see her father and the cowman striding through the great herd in the evening sun – 'head 'em up and move 'em out' – was to place her in a cattle-drive in the classic film *Red River*, John Wayne and Montgomery Clift locked in an oedipal feud on the Chisholm Trail. Homespun tents rigged up between the garden cottonwoods, holey tarps age-stained the colour of dried tobacco leaves, soon became covered wagons. Farmhands on the distant ridgelines were noble Sioux, honest injuns, restless as seed-heavy tumbleweed. Old ropes were lariats and sometimes also rattlesnakes, coiling out of the brambly chaparral. Even the amiable grime-coated coalman took on the form of Jack Palance, the black-gloved hired gun from *Shane*, a stone-hearted killer…

Mum enjoys the fifty-minute arc of *Wagon Train*, pleased she'd recognised the guest actor Brandon de Wilde, the kid from *Shane*, now a slender, querulous young man. She hears the slow heavy tread of her father coming down the stairs – he'll be wanting the News. She turns off the lamp and a bar of the fire, straightens the redundant antimacassar on the back of the couch and slips into the cold kitchen to make a cup of tea. Like Shane, her question is whether to stay or whether to go. Her sonless father works her hard, and she has equalled anything a son could have done, though she is scarce recognised for it. She's been driving tractors since the age of ten, and milking, raking, baling, gleaning, feeding, tending, shifting, digging, herding, all hours, all weathers. Hauling out the tree stumps on this patch of land is the devil's own job. She is suffocated with the dust of cultivation. The farmlands are no longer a mythic playground, more a hardscrabble republic of loneliness. She looks long at her reflection in the dark window, interlaced with the falling snow outside. The kitchen clock seems to have gained again, fifteen minutes at least. Holding the mug of tea, she can feel the calluses on her hands, but it's not easy to up and ride on through to the next valley.

In the morning she is out soon after first light, while the yellow sky is tinted with long contours of relic white. The farm cats twist around her legs as she closes the gate and sets off to walk a mile through the village, its lanes for weeks gnawed by ice. By the time she reaches the bus stop at the Black Boy pub, the local farmers have been out in cab-less tractors, clearing the sloping road up from the A1. Her knees, covered only with thin nylon stockings, are beginning to chap and her hands are coldly clasping her change purse. On the bus to town, the usually droning diesel engines baffled by the weather, she sits alone near the front, and peers out of the misted windows at the blankness outside. Often the morning trips to work at the valuers and auctioneers are also curdled with a fog like gun smoke, and the day will already seem in tatters. She smiles at the other wan teenagers on the bus, most of whom she's always known. They know her as a quiet one, but not to be trifled with – the boys in the little village school who had poured slugs and worms over her head long remembered her answering clout, even though they'd never admit they had gone home that day weeping. She'll give them an old-fashioned look even now. It is still something of an adventure to travel into town. Down the busy High Street, she looks back on the rare trips out with her father as a child, to the pictures or to wrestling bouts, and once, in her smart kilt skirt, to see the antics of Norman Wisdom at the Empire Theatre, her father, not a man given to laughter, crying with hilarity. As the bus stops, despite herself, she is already thinking of the journey home after work, when she will close her eyes in the mechanical light and listen to the shift of gears and the slow whirr of the wipers, soon to be back in the snow-sagging village, the snug of sisters at home.

A short time later she met my father, a small-town maverick, who impressed her with his ability to jump the queue and get the best seats at the picture house – he knew all the ushers and could call in small favours. Growing up, Mum would gift me a love of the western too. It was one of our many plots of common ground, and still is. It never mattered how often we saw John Wayne battle his demons in *The Searchers* or Kirk Douglas handle his chestnut mare with cool ease in *Lonely are the Brave* or Gary Cooper face down the Miller gang in *High Noon*, with the living room curtains half-drawn, we were rapt with the onscreen drama, each corralled to a quiet outlaw spirit. Today I still think of my mother as a frontierswoman, a clear-sighted Willa Cather heroine on the 'the shaggy grass country' of the prairies, uprooted to the tangle-hedged fields of eastern England. She has the true grit of a woman born to hard work, though the sight of Gregory Peck in *The Big Country*, a displaced sea-captain in the canyons of the West, will see her give that broad gap-toothed smile, the thought that her ship will come in yet. To see her laugh and play with my children, her grandchildren, her loving kindness and self-effacing wish for them to be her centre point, is to know she still makes a Garden out of the Desert. She has all the pioneer qualities, honestly come by. She knows the country, all the names of the plants in her garden and in the hedgerow. She is fascinated by birds and is a sage of weather lore. She's good with animals, but is an unsentimental wrangler. She is the keeper of the homestead and our Rock of all Ages. Willa Cather once wrote of a friend: 'She is one of the truest artists I ever knew in the keenness and sensitiveness of her enjoyment, in her love of people and her willingness to take pains.' Words so true of my mother.

1979

Milestone Inspectors

The old man had told me often enough about South Africa and the Great War and life in the King's Own, so when the county recruiting board came to Gonerby village hall in the autumn of 1939, there I was lining up with all the other fellows. Just past twenty-three, not long married and a young'un still on gripe water at home, in those days I was delivering bread on my bike every morning before the sun had warmed my hands, with only a slice of Mother's Pride and a dog-end Capstan to get me going. The morning had been proper rough, rain coming down in an onding, as Mam used to say, heavy enough to bow Parker's shop canopy to the floor. I remember my overalls had been soaked through and the bicycle clip had left a rusty welt round my shins. I got out of my wet things when I got home and left them hanging by the range fire, put on my Sunday suit and, with a lick and a promise, left to meet Alec and Joe by the memorial cross. We larked about a bit, looking up at the clock face on St Sebastian's church and thinking about pelting a few stones at it, and eyeing the black crow that someone had tamed to land on folks' heads. Mostly though we just drew on fags and talked about the football last Saturday, when Bob Seneschal had his leg broken in the first half of the village cup game.

Soon enough, St Sebastian's clock had us down the road, side by side, in time, marching like. We saw a few other fellows going in the village hall, including old Charlie Wright, who had been in the last war, and he must have been over forty. We were made to stand up straight and answer to our names read by this bristly bloke behind the makeshift desk they used as the beer counter at weddings. The bloke had a thick North Riding croak and I remembered when Dad took us for a day out after Granny died and we went to Gaping Gill – big enough down there to fit the whole of Lincoln Cathedral in it, he'd said. After a bit, the military doctor came along the line of us, tapping our knees, getting us to bend over and cough, and then checking our chests with a cold steel stethoscope. It was all we could do not to crease up laughing. It made us feel like we were nippers in school again. But when it came to me, I felt like a badger dug out for the hounds and brimming little soughs of sweat came seeping down my nose. I could hear the cawing of some late-leaving rooks in the big elm in Green Lane and wondered if we were in for more hard wind and rain. The doctor didn't say anything but scribbled some notes on a pad and the sergeant-major type tapped me on the shoulder and steered me out. His words flew at me straight: *You better get fitted up for a coffin, mate.* I saw the open door and a low black swoop of rainclouds. Forty years on, I still remember a solitary hooded crow wheeling over the valley head beyond.

Dad could never credit it, me failing the army medical. Reckoned it was crackpot. But I had learned from school days, when the headmistress used her ringed fingers like a knuckleduster, to keep my head down, work hard, get on with it, and I think Dad respected me for it in the end. He was always such a tough bugger, a small man but ox-strong and hard as hornbeam. After a drink, he'd tell you all about his war, Natal 1900, bayoneting Boer farmers as soon as looking at them. The sound of butchered flesh was like flensed blubber, he said, though he must have got that from a Grimsby whaler, I reckon. Even when he fell off the hay cart, past eighty, and the prong of the pitchfork went through his ear, he got himself patched up and back working in the vetch fields the next day. Every Saturday night he'd be in the pub, only leaving his pint pot to break up the street fights our Tony used to get into. With his cordon of cronies sat around the fire, he would lean at the bar, talking like all the hands hereabouts, with his mouth hardly open, the words all measured out in a slow slur, a habit picked up from the auction ring at the cattle market. And he walked everywhere, always Shanks' pony, a right footslogger, like he was still on some route march on the Highveld. Straight-backed and an even tread, his short wiry frame covered the four-mile round trip to Hornsby's foundry every day. Even on Sundays he'd step out down the lane towards the grange and the rail line running past Jericho Wood, as he'd say, 'Just to go there and back to see how far it was.'

I remember when he finally started catching the bus to work, sitting at the back, the stem of his pipe clamped in his mouth with his last remaining black tooth. That day Arnie Field jolted him going down the bus aisle, and knocked Dad's last tooth clean out. Arnie was always a bit frit of him, like many folks, and shied away, expecting a thump. But Dad just said, 'By guy, thanks mate, been wanting that out for a long time.' Had everyone falling about in the tap room of the Recruiting Sergeant, that one. At home, of course, he ruled the roost, such as it was in that mouldy old house, kept our Mam out of sight, hard set to. No, he was never one to jib at a scrap, though he credited me with being the brains of the family and knew I wasn't like him, not built for strong-arming.

It all dims. I can't really bring back his face now and I have no pictures of him. It's twenty-odd years since he went, fading away like old soldiers are supposed to. The bugger lived to eighty-five, a stroke robbing his speech at the end, though he could still sing hymns, spare and haunting, sat in the armchair in the Pond Street house he'd been born in. Funny what you remember. When I was young, he'd stand, straight as the regimental flagstaff, in front of the hearth, warming his hands and the seat of his overalls on the fire. On the mantelpiece behind were always newly starched shirt collars and the stud, and a packet of fags. Along with my brother Joe, we loved looking at the little printed masterpieces on the cigarette boxes: the bearded sailor on Player's Navy Cut, the battleships on Senior Service. On a fancy occasion, there might be Peter Stuyvesant's, with its coat of arms. One or two fags would be pushed up proud of the packet, ready for taking – our Joe used to cut them off near the tip and push back the ends in the box to disguise what he had done; until our Mam cottoned on, and just gave him a few to smoke.

Anyway, I reckon I was lucky not to join up and be sent off to the war like my brother-in-law Frank, and go through all that. I stayed at home and the war came to me. I was the air-raid warden and fireman around the bridge and the big mills and maltings at the bottom of Somerby Hill. It seemed like they bombed us every night in the early years of war, when we were really up against it. The explosions lit up the black river waters, the smoking houses and factories, the railway yards blown to hell. I'd be fire-watching at St Wulfram's or checking up on the blackout, inspecting the shelters or lugging gasmasks about. Or I'd be going up the ladder against a tottering wall looking to get folks out of bombed-out houses, mouth full of hot dust. Ernie Taylor, my next-door neighbour, would hold the steps – I never felt safe with anybody else doing it. And it was a bad job when it was people you knew, buried in the rubble. Especially the kids.

On my day off I started driving an ambulance, and I was never short of a job. Even when I started work in the Lipton's shop there was no let-up in war work. My hours were full with the worry of it. The missus got caught out one time in a daylight raid while she was out shopping. I got her and the kids into the basement storeroom that ran under the road to meet the cellars of the Red Lion opposite. They had to sit on rattling crates of empty bottles, listening to the rumbling and booming above, plaster falling in from the low ceiling like split bags of flour. A bottle of whisky someone had hidden away down there smashed on the flagstones, and when they eventually staggered out from underground, dazed and dusty, they all had thick heads and a raging thirst.

Most days, I'd be out on the van, doling out the slim rations. Given I had some education, folks would get me to fill in forms or check bills or the pools coupons. Sometimes I'd read out the official telegrams – bad news mostly – or write letters to the blokes serving abroad. The roaming scribe, the parson at Bitchfield called me. Hard days, though I know there were many who had it a lot worse, and feel the weight of it even now.

After the war, I went back to Gonerby three times a week, to give Dad a shave and haircut and listen to him cursing the factory bosses. This'll make you laugh: I used to deliver to the big house at Hungerton and once I went into the kitchen there and the under-butler, a former Italian prisoner of war, was plucking a goose. The job was too hard, the quills too long, so he lathered the bird with shaving cream and shaved it with a cutthroat razor. Doubt it made a good dinner. Anyway, from him I got to know how to do the shaving job very neat and Dad always wanted me to do it. One time, Joe had to stand in for me, but his motorbike accident had left him with a tremor and he cut Dad's face to ribbons. Never happened again. So, though I've always liked to talk, I became Dad's silent barber. And something more, the son who would listen, take it all in, take it to heart, and try to understand, not catching his eye too often in the mirror, as he sat there in his vest, tilting his jaw. I can bring back the smell of it now, those times, while I was stropping the razor on the calf's tongue: embrocation and hair oils and such jollop. And I remember how as he bent his head forward so as I could snip his hair at the nape, he'd often admire my shoes – I've always liked to be well shod – the feather patterns and pin-prick whorls on the uppers, always shined to perfection: 'You can see yer face in them boots,' he'd say, running his hand over his now bristleless chin. Afterwards, I'd go out into the yard for a smoke and look out over the crinkle-crankle wall of the big house and out towards the low moor. There always seemed to be these brown-dappled moths, like smudges, on the riddled door to the lean-to, clinging on in the creeping wind. Like I said, funny what you remember.

Things are mostly better these days, though the wife has been gone these last three years, and I do miss her a good deal. She was twelve years older than me, and spent up her youth looking after a large household of younger brothers. I think she had resigned herself to becoming an old maid until she went to see a fortune-teller at the Mid Lent Fair. 'You'll meet a man in uniform,' she was told, 'and you'll marry him.' Soon after, I turned up at the doorstep at Belvoir Avenue in my trainee baker's get-up and that was that! Now I look after our little house – I'm a home bird, always have been. I've packed up the van shop. I liked the driving work, and got to know folks in all the villages for miles around. People come up to me in the street now, remembering when they were youngsters, starved for treats – I'd hand out broken biscuits and sweets, and swap tins of peaches for farm eggs and butter. One old boy the other day reminded me of the time I turned up in Swayfield covered in porridge after a wet bag of oats had split on the side shelf. Most folks have cars these days and can get to the big places in town, and Lipton's said the van got too dear to run, so I'm on the shop floor now, stuck inside with a brown coat on, trying to keep out the way.

Sundays, I like to go out with the grandkids. We often drive north and end up at Culverthorpe, for a walk around the twin lakes in front of the manor house. This is the place, on hot summer days. The paths are shady and the water is made for stone-skimming. We like to spot birds too, the dragon heads of grebes out on the open water and the slow herons, stalking in the shallows. The boys will run about among the big felled oaks around the shoreline, kicking the shingle or playing at soldiers, looking for Germans in the ruined trees. One time, summer just gone it was, we found a real one. He was past the boathouse, sitting on the ground near the causeway between the lakes, drying off in the sun after a long dip in the east lake. I knew him a long time and he wasn't a bad chap. He was an old POW, originally from the Baltic coast, he told me once. He must have been younger than me, but he'd been living out for years and his lean face was burnt dark and rough as soot. His hair was long and grey-streaked, but he was always close-shaved, and he wore a dark corduroy tie and a white shirt, frayed but near clean. His greatcoat had seen better days though, the holey pockets stuffed with odds and ends. He produced his cigarette lighter from a patch on the inside liner, a little brass disc with an old coin stamped into the side. He told me he had fashioned it while stuck in a desert cave in North Africa, in the weeks before he was captured by the Eighth Army. For many years now, he'd tramped all over England and Wales, west to east and back again, going on and on down a corridor of his own imagining. You'd see him, odd times, loping down the road, his hazel stick in hand, a rough canvas bag on his back, a dinted enamel billycan hooked on a loop. Free as a bird, he said he was. That day at the lake, he must have had some new boots lately. I noticed they had not got much wear, not for a milestone inspector, as Dad would have called him. Something about the German fellow's hatched hazel eyes reminded me of the old man.

He had made a sort of bird-scrape in the gravel to lie in, lined with compressed feathers, mud, beech leaves. His cracked hands were grimy, as he kept digging them into the thin soil by his side. A haze of gnats buzzed around his head but he didn't seem to notice. He said he'd just come up from Rutland reservoir, camping out in a hollow near to the shore at Normanton church. He liked watery places, he said. He could peel off his togs and be swimming out, resting his knees, healing up his feet, all buoyed up like. Somebody told me he'd once been in Rauceby, at the asylum. No doubt he'd seen a lot in the war years, and since then, he'd been traipsing the back roads for years on end, sometimes close to sleep while on the march. He told me he walked with all the voices from long ago, but they fell into murmurs he could hardly hear now. The boys were a bit frit of him and kept their distance, but I reckoned he was just a sad fellow who couldn't get home.

1970
Klondike

Harold strikes the match against the box and cups the flame from the wind. The match goes out and he tries again, his hands a little unsteady. He leans over one of the larger funerary monuments in the graveyard. The match blows out again, and Harold remembers his father's superstition against 'third lights', a sniper's target in the trenches of the Great War. Soon, though, he has the Woodbine lit and he breathes in deeply, and picks up the mug of tea resting on a table memorial. Expelling the smoke from the side of his mouth, he puts the matches back in the pocket of his fustian work jacket, hung on a long-handled spade dug into the earth. Although Harold has worked up a sweat, it is a bleak day in a marrow-cold January. They say it's as cold as the grave, but Harold knows it to be warmer in the ground than it is exposed on these treeless heights.

The hard surface rings when he drives the spade in. There is a scent of darkness, rising from the hillside that sweeps down to the cemetery. Harold can just make out the sooty outline of the Ruston's engine factory down London Road, the kilns of the maltings behind, and the clank and smoke of the railyards near Station Road, much less these days since the end of the steam trains. The needle-point tower of the crematorium is lost somewhere over towards the Harrowby Land Settlement, where Harold's uncles struggled to found smallholdings after the First World War. A gravel-eyed jackdaw hurtles down the side of a stone wall and lifts a cigarette butt from behind a wooden gate.

'Bloody ground's too hard to shovel,' Harold says to himself. 'And he was a big bugger, the bloke going in this hole.' All the years he's been digging graves here, it never gets easy. Not that difficult either, mind. No one bothers him much out here. Odd times he'll see the sexton, beetling along like billy-o, but he never says much. The parson will nod on the way to the Barley Mow, his sackcloth rumpling. Always thirsty. Harold will put his hand up and holler, 'Now then Reverend, are you winning?' and Harold will know how the red-faced cleric feels: 'My belly thinks my throat's been cut.' But another hour of this digging, and Harold will be at the bar-room of the White Horse too, along with the Giant, Vincent Swarby, near seven feet tall and known to drink a pint of beer every quarter of an hour, sixteen in a session. Harold can't match that, but he likes his company. He never looks at Harold 'all-gone-out', not like some in the starchy saloon bar with their airs and graces, scorning his lack of education. 'Some of 'em think we're all green as bleddy cabbages round here, and as thick too. But I won't let them upskittle me,' thinks Harold.

Harold throws the fag-end in the grave he has now half-dug and takes off his cap to scratch the top of his head. His short military-cut hair is ashy and coarse, like flaked tobacco. His eyebrows, thick and unruly, are glistening and a thin vapour rises off his back to mingle with the last of the Woodbine smoke. He sips his tea, so strong and sweet that he coughs. 'Has it got bones in it?' he says to himself. He looks over the Victorian necropolis. A few florid monuments, but most are simple stones and crosses, grey and uneven, forgotten as dolmen. 'Touch wood, I'll never be superstitious.' Harold likes to pick out the muted green lichens in stony nooks with his fingernails, now stained and ridged as a washboard. He shivers. He's wearing two pairs of thick socks against the cold, but his boots are a touch too big for him and his toes are numb. It's inching towards Saturday afternoon – time for a pint, then time for a sleep.

A robin now sits on the spade. Harold knows him well; he's a constant companion, a tough little prospector, scanning his province, his song sharp and high. Harold has looked out for him since finding his moss-lined nest in an old pail in the tool shed last spring. No, it's not a bad job, he thinks. Had worse. It's a well-worn thread of thought for Harold these days, to review his sundry career. The tough days before the war, during the Depression, when work was hard to come by. He spent a year up in the Scunthorpe ironworks, long hours at the forge, whelmed in sweat, punishing work that left him blackened head to toe, his work togs softened and saponified like axle grease. He found then he would take any work to get by. When he was working at the open-cast mine in Nottinghamshire, he'd keep his motorbike, oily and fumy, in the kitchen at home. He remembers how his brother Jack's wife Evelyn, always one to think herself a cut above, would complain. She gave him his nickname, 'Klondike', him always ruckled and grimy, but ever on the go, expecting to strike gold. He would give it her back: 'You want to git, you bloody goshawp!' He liked the company of his fellow workers, hardened men like himself, desperate for employment. One time at the ironworks, his mate the fireman had just been paid his week's wages, and put the brown packet of cash in the top pocket of his shirt. As he was shovelling fuel into the furnace, the packet fell out of the pocket onto the blade and then carried through straight into the fire. All his money burnt up in an instant. He was distraught: how would he pay his rent? But the men did a whip-round and replaced the wages between them. Comradeship was worth more than the promise of gold.

Eventually laid off, Harold came home again and landed a plum job as a bus conductor, playful and wisecracking with the passengers as he passed down the long, packed aisle. He was doing well now, kitting himself out in posh double-breasted suits – 'dressed like a lord', his dad said. The old man suspected he was twisting the bus company, pocketing some of the fares, but Harold never let on, and his dad was forced to let it go: 'I'll believe you, but thousands wouldn't.'

Soon after he was dismissed by the bus company, but Harold began again, driving the borough tipping lorry, delivering sand and gravel for highway repairs on the metalled trunk roads of the southwest of the county. On his day off he drove an ambulance part-time. Once he was in the North, delivering an empty vehicle, and reached Halifax as the factories were letting out, the narrow, cobbled streets crowded with pushbikes and bone-weary mill hands. Harold swore, rang the ambulance's clanging roof bell and got through the town in no time at all, thanking God he wasn't a factory-grafter like the poor sods left staggering in the wake of his exhaust smoke.

Harold empties the dregs of tea over the mound of earth at his feet and steps down into the part-dug grave. A pit for winter's tribute, the crop of the old and the unfortunate. The soil gives off a tarry whiff, its consistency hard as a caulking iron. He starts digging again, soon regaining a work pulse, ignoring the pull in his back. The robin has landed in the spoil heap, probing and alert as ever, an eye for the main chance. As the bird dips to land a worm, his white rump lifts in the air and deposits a small pale turd into the hole. Harold thinks of the pits like this he dug in the sandier soils of North Africa, when he was in the army medical unit during the war. He had preferred it in the catering corps, a soft job he thought, frying eggs and bacon on upturned manhole covers, joking with the NCOs. Mainly he likes to forget about the bloody war though – too many folks still bang on about it to this day, and it's a time best done and gone.

Thin sunlight lances down into the pit and Harold squints, stopping for a moment. It's a long season till his summer holidays. He always goes to Betws-y-Coed in the mountain valleys of North Wales. He will hitch his homemade trailer to the car and in the trailer will be a rough canvas tent and his fireside armchair from the best room at home. Tomorrow, months away from the long days of June and July, he'll strip his car to bits and clean the 'old gel', all in readiness for the annual trip. The hub cabs will be old saucepan lids, polished to gleaming. The tyres will be long since new, reclaimed from an old wreck at the destructor yard. He laughs at the memory of when brother-in-law Bob went away with them in his ancient Austen Seven, its narrow-gauge wheels getting stuck in the tramlines at Llandudno. But, the holidays are a long way off, and thinking about them won't get the job done.

Even so, Harold looks at his watch. He reaches up for the snap tin, and finds a last sandwich. Fish paste. Keep the hunger off until he can get to his beer. He decides it is time to pack up and hauls himself out of the grave and knocks the dirt off the spade end. Another house built to last till Doomsday. His jacket draped on his arm, he walks to the tool shed, clamped to the cemetery wall. The vicar says the shed is like Harold's anchorhold, his steadying place, where he can retreat, give ground, and get some thinking done, but Harold isn't well versed in the habits of medieval hermits, and thinks the vicar is soft as grease. He puts away the spade, moths fluttering out of the dark corners, and swirls out his mug in water from the standpipe. He sits on the slatted chair, wipes dirt off his trouser legs, dowses his hands in a jar of tea-brown water and then rubs his reddened palms together, thinking of the first draught of ale. Time was he'd drink with his brother R.J. at the White Horse on a Saturday afternoon, meeting him on his way down from the allotments. But R.J. has been gone two years now, and lies buried halfway up the slope towards the Hills and Hollows.

Rowland Joseph. How the teasing head-scarfed girls had flocked to him when he was a young fellow on his stall outside the munitions factory, such a fine-looking boy, his dark hair swept back on a high forehead, his face nut-brown, his green-eyed gaze steady and disarming. He had worked in the market gardens with their father in the fields off Kitty Briggs Lane. As a youngster R.J. had a capacity for mischief that never left him. Once he was with his father delivering potatoes on the pony and trap to Belton army camp during the Great War. Though he was only seven years old he had a deep gruff voice and when they passed by a squad of soldiers at drill, he shouted 'Halt!' The troops duly came to attention and the sergeant wasn't long lost for words. His dad was furious – 'You could have got us shot!' – but R.J. was never constrained by authority. He was another in the family of fine horse-handlers. He was also another of the family hard drinkers, a real toper. It got him in the end. He had already narrowly avoided a pile up on the high street when driving the horse and cart home and putting his hand out at the junction to indicate left, the horse having more sense to carry straight on. At the crossroads, he would regularly tip the hat off the traffic policeman, cantering off with the copper's shouts trailing behind him. Slowly, he started to lose all reason, a run-in with the Income Tax playing obsessively on his mind, all worsened by the drink. He spent some time in Rauceby mental hospital. There he wrote, over and again, to the Revenue, trying to heal, but lost in an incoherent, repeating chant, an echolalia. When released he turned on his best pal, brother-in-law Bob, sawing off the leg of the antique chair that Bob would sit on in R.J.'s kitchen. A crippling attack of paranoia in the field next to the fire station followed – Bob had tried to give him a soothing cigarette but R.J. yelled out, 'It's poisoned, you're all trying to poison me.' He tried to put the fag in a horse's mouth – 'Look, the bloody oss won't even smoke it!'

And so, the steady fall to mental illness. It was said he scared his mother to a fatal heart attack, and then threw her clothes out of the window and into the street. Of course, in the family none of it was ever talked about, hushed up in tight knots of shame. He died alone at home, aged just fifty-seven, the police having to break in, finding him in the chair, his hand over his chest as if in mortal pain. Harold had cried like he hadn't since he was a roaring child, and now spends a few moments every week tending the grave, clearing away the snarling brambles, scooping off the marly dust.

Harold sets off for the pub, hunched in his coat, his gait stiff, but tap-room thoughts propelling him along. The trees along Harrowby Road are as stripped as antlers and he notices the robin on a long branch like a fingerpost, seeing him off. The thirst ups his pace. He used to brew his own ale, and bring out the flagons on Sundays with the family when he'd sing in his light tenor voice to his sister May's piano accompaniment. One Sunday dinner though the pressurised cork popped out of the bottle – he must have left it to ferment too long – and it hit him in the eye, sending him purblind. Now he prefers the windy company of the White Horse, the ceaseless supping of the Giant, the carnival of upset domino tiles and arrowing darts, the shiftless walls of smoke, the laughter that follows all his well-honed tales. Life can be sweet even for rum 'un like him, thinks Harold, and he crosses over the road, dust and clumps of earth loosing off his boots.

Frank, the young artilleryman, 1940s

Watercolour of Frank, by German POW F. Buchholz, Kiel, 1945

Frank's father, Joseph, late 19th century

Frank's Lipton's shop, 1960s

My mother, early 1960s

Grandad serving in the mobile shop, Bitchfield, 1959

Grandad Sentance, Mablethorpe, 1950s

Florrie, standing second left, with her Dorset family, 1950s

August and Kate

August leading a séance, 1920s

Kate, 1890s

The Harrisons outside a pub, late 19th century

Page from Kate's album

Grandad and Dad, Mablethorpe, 1947

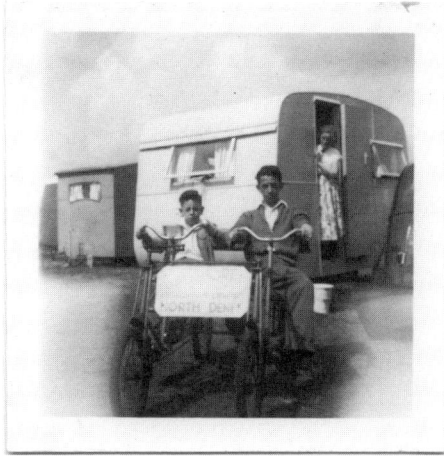

Dad, Granny and Grandad on holiday in Norfolk, 1950s

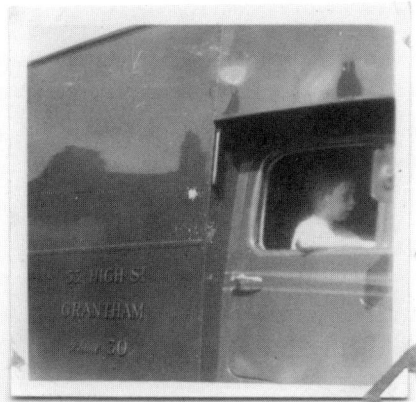

Dad, keen learner, early 1950s

Dad the cyclist, 1958

Dad and friend, 1959

Dad, on the road, 1960s

Dad, always behind the wheel, 1961

Footballers, Noorderplantsoen, Groningen, 1990

Francesca, in my student room, Groningen, 1990

Groningen, autumn 1990

Het Pakhuis pub, Groningen, 1990

With Francesca, dinner at the ISH, Groningen, 1990

Farewell dinner, Groningen, 1990

1946

Blood Will Tell

Late in the first August after the war, and the sun was newly up over the flattened acres of reaped barley. Florrie watched the sky as she walked over the courtyard cobbles from Goosegate farmhouse to the washhouse, a bundle of sheets and shirts under her arm. It had long been her daybreak instinct to inspect the patterns of clouds, the feel of the air, the behaviour of birds. It would be another hot day, slow-banked and close. The early light was still deadbeat, a thin battered gold now uncovering the hard ground of unswept dust, the honeyed stone, the climbing shrubs, the brittle-leafed trees and the painted fences. And though the whirling cadre of swifts had now gone south, the first ushers of autumn were a week or more off yet.

Florrie had other burdens. Fred, her husband of twenty-five years, had been attacked by a bull in the riverfield the week before and had died of his injuries later that same day. The funeral was to be in a few days. Family from far and wide and businessmen and dignitaries from all the local farmers' associations would be in attendance, to observe the rites, to pay respects and, amongst themselves, to assess the new lay of the land. Florrie felt little in her slow-beat heart but steeliness. She walked through the days as if in a void. Amid the shock, Florrie had viewed his hard white-marbled body at the mortuary and allowed herself to wonder where had the love once grown. Was it lost long ago amongst the choke of thistles and the clinging burdock in this grit-rasped parish? She felt the days, months and years of her life at the farm were stacked like old hay in the barn. The account books were left blank of the unthanked toil, the betrayals, the indignations. Her regard for him had dried up like a downed bird. She would endure, as she had endured the ragged fiction of their marriage, and the funeral would be the first public declaration of that fact. But now it was Monday, unvaryingly wash day, beginning and ending in hours of darkness.

Florrie could not abide laziness. She worked and worked and expected all around to do the same. If, as they say, happiness was to be attained through the meld of love and work, she would try to compensate the lack of the one with the excess of the other. Not that happiness was her stated goal. For her that was something on the far shore. The sum of each day was the amount of work achieved – perhaps an inherited fear of the humiliation of the workhouse. To be idle was unknown and unknowable, and though she might huff and puff at the laxity of others, she performed her own work without a sigh. In this way work became her religion, the sacraments of which were contained in this house and yard, and the hundred or so acres of productive land it served.

Florrie paused a moment at the door to the washhouse, a small brick building beyond the coalhouse and the outside lavatory. Later that day her sons were to slaughter a pig in the place where the pigs were always slaughtered, the makeshift shambles against the whitewashed laundry wall, palely splattered yet with old stains and now licked at by the torpid farm dog. She checked that she had remembered to bring out the wooden tray to catch the blood for black pudding; Florrie would also prepare the corpse, de-bristle the pigskin, and take the head to make brawn. The wake would call for all this.

Not yet fifty, Florrie carried the trace of long years of hard work. Her once coppery hair was greying, swept back in unfussy waves from her flat forehead. Her eyes were pale, watchful, a little sunken and tired. She had a broad mouth, capable of a full grin like her father's, but more often lost in the clench of her good teeth, though she had a habit of grinding them in her sleep. Her once shapely frame had become sturdy and round-shouldered, her arms solid and welted with old cuts and burns. Her build might have been of a stock-handler or no-nonsense village publican. There was a thin gold band on her ring finger, but she wore no other ornament, no frippery. She had an air of stern intelligence, and gave away few hints of buried dreams.

Sunlight streaked through the small grimy window to the laundry. The configuration of the washhouse told of Florrie's work on countless wash days, the arrangement of the tubs, the grooved floor now discoloured with smudges like old whey, the polished tools hanging on nails on the wall, and the precise homes for the starch, bleach and laundry blue, all within easy reach for her weekly routine. She lit the fire beneath the big copper standing in its brick recess. Normally she'd have done this an hour before dawn, but now she was no longer pressed by hard-voiced demands, and the household agendas were hers. At the dolly tub she began to agitate the dirty clothes with tongs, working with her shoulders, her strong hands wrenching out the dirt, her knuckles showing through like flint. After a while, wiping her brow, she pulled out the washing to be wrung and dried in the mangle outside, always with elaborate care of her fingers.

Then she hung everything on the line, strung between two silvery apple trees, with gypsy pegs, wresting the sheets like mainsails fore and aft, pinning the shirts in graceful, fluid manoeuvres, for optimal exposure to sun and breeze – she would be thankful for a drying day. Later, back inside, she would press the clean clothes with a sadiron heated on the range, then to be folded and put away. The cycle continued throughout the day, load after load of sheets, shirts, overalls, the fabric of the household scrubbed, cleaned, made anew. It was the drudgery of all Mondays, but today it felt right to be doing this. Her late husband's shirts were done with the rest.

At six she went back to the kitchen. She would soon need to start breakfast. From the larder she gathered up thick strips of their own bacon, fresh-laid eggs, flour-dusted loaves of white bread baked the night before. Her sons and daughter, in their early twenties and fierce hungry, would be soon up for a day of chores or in the harvest fields – at mealtimes their eyes were never bigger than their bellies and they 'could eat a horse behind the saddle'. She could hear the Italian farmhands, two small middle-aged men displaced by the war and bound to unending graft by Fred, emerging from the cramped attic room, their worn-out work boots clattering on the back staircase. The farm rhythms continued, even in the shadow of a death.

The dead man had been a giant in these parts, his bulk standing out among the crookbacked labourers of the Lincoln Edge. Six feet tall and broad with it, Fred was a heavy man in a coarse tweed jacket that was never rumpled or ragged. At rest, he had barely seemed his forty-nine years; but his usual self-assured stride had lately told of a slowing down, some creeping arthritis of the lower joints. He spoke rarely, with a conversational habit of raising his head slightly, a weighing up while he looked down the length of that broken bristly nose. His words were mainly to command: in the field or at the workshop or in the slaughterhouse; at the kitchen table; barkingly, at the bar of the Black Horse Inn; or later on, in the upstairs room. Florrie had once been swept away by his grand gestures, his ambition, a hushed pride residing in her chest. But for years now she had quietly moved around him, alert, studious, solicitous and anticipatory. Their younger son, Jack, avoided him, and would hide in the hay loft, nursing his wheezy chest, or find an undisturbed hedgerow under which to lie and read – Fred had thought him a useless article. It was the elder son, Ted, who had faced him with boldness; and when Fred was riled by him, until the day Ted matched him in size, he would be free with the strap.

Florrie remembered a Sunday cricket game, before the war. She had stopped a moment in the long grass and hay rattle at the north field edge to watch. Fred was the impassive umpire, standing like a monument at the bowler's end; young Ted was in the infield, cocky and unconcerned, his hands in his pockets. The batsman had hit a fierce cut-shot and Ted had been hit full in the face. He had staggered forward, his blood spilling on a good length, a red weal rising on his cheekbone. Fred had then dragged him off, berating Ted for his inattention. Everyone had looked away. Someone had fetched the sawdust and spread it over the bloody patch. The game had resumed in near silence, the wind murmuring through the damson trees. Florrie had hurried home in the attempt to intervene, but if Fred ever seemed bidden, he never was. He had thought himself a man of substance, outfitted in broadcloth and well-breeched, a swaggering village Caesar. And it seemed to Florrie that his cruelty had been matched by his own cruel end.

In the kitchen Florrie stretched her aching back against the sink and from the sleeve of her smock plucked out some oil-black thunderflies, the tiny feathery-winged thrips that plagued the farm at harvest time. There was still more work ahead than behind her, but she felt as restless as an ill-sitting hen. From the dresser she brought down the teacups – rarely used – that she had been given by the household staff when she left the employ of the Mansion House in the City of London. How long ago that seemed. Though she had lived with her aunt in suburban Eltham while in service at the Lord Mayor's residence, for her London was a walled vision of fascination, a gilded glimpse of the sumptuous lives of the great and the good. But after a year or two she had moved to Lincolnshire, convinced by her cousin who had married a soldier stationed in the county. She became the cook at the big house at Caythorpe, on the heathland cut through by the ancient Roman road of Ermine Street. It was there, soon after the end of the First World War, that she had met Fred, lately discharged from the Royal Artillery, and now a young butcher delivering to the house several times a week. She had accepted him and he had wasted no time in sealing the bargain. He'd travelled down to Eltham to Florrie's aunt and gifted a box of meat to sweeten the marriage deal. Then he'd cycled to Florrie's hometown, Lyme Regis on the southwest coast, to ask formally for her hand, following the route of the old Fosse Way through the soft limestone belt running down the country from Lincolnshire through Northamptonshire and Oxfordshire, the Cotswolds and Somerset to the ancient shore at Lyme. His mind was set, his purpose clear; he rested on the way in pubs and at field edges, making a travelling survey of the farms of southern England. After two hundred and fifty miles and a short distance from her parents' house, his bike had a puncture. He had changed the tyre at the Hunter's Lodge inn on the Dorset and Devon border, using a water trough to source the leak, afterwards taking a glass or two of strong cider in the saloon bar, before carrying on down the sunless sunken lanes towards the bay. This had become the stuff of family legend of course, but Florrie now found that even the memory of this display of supreme conviction annoyed her. It seemed she had little say in the decisions, then or since. This had not been the way of her own parents, who'd brought up all nine of them, including the girls, to develop thick seams of independence. But there had been no brooking Fred, and Florrie had had to find the nous to handle him.

Fred's father had bought them Goosegate Farm in 1921. Soon Fred proved to be a pinch-penny and money-hoarder, rarely shelling out other than on his epic drinking and carousing in the local inns on Saturday nights. His girth expanded with his bank balance. Ribald drinkers in the bar-rooms said he'd skin a fart for a farthing. And, drifting to her ears in queues for the bus or from idle talk in the village shop, were rumours of his infidelities, with barmaids, war widows, even with Florrie's two younger unmarried sisters, and there were whispers of misbegotten children scattered across the district, three with the landlady at Marston pub. Once Ted went to the saw mill at Bennington, and was mistaken for his ringer from Fulbeck, a half-brother he had no knowledge of.

She worried for Ted. He'd set himself as a bulwark, but more and more he was his father's son. She couldn't fault his industry – last winter he had hand-dug a culvert from the stack yard to the field, and then sunk and brick-lined a deep well down to the water table, thinking little of the risk of drowning during its construction. But his harshness could turn to violence. She was thinking of Emil, the German POW, who had been detailed to work in the lucerne fields. Ted and the cowman Horace had been talking by the field edge, both swearing for a solid half hour and never saying the same thing twice. They could see Emil had got his cart stuck in a track rut, and was whipping the horse, cursing in his own language. Ted had run out and climbed on the cart board and punched the German on the jaw. Emil was knocked to the ground and then ran off back to Allington prison camp. Ted, beef-strong and fuelled by fury, had hoisted the cart out of the hole by himself, the full weight on his iron shoulders. And another time there had been the tramp who had slept in a full hay barn and lit a cigarette – Ted had belted him too, and ran him off the property.

She would watch him at the breakfast table, gathering the crumbs on the table after the meal with his rough, freckled hands, a tidy man, wasting nothing. They had done well out of the war, licitly and otherwise – Fred had said they hadn't wanted the fighting to end. Florrie knew he had the small pails used to feed weaning calves stuffed with banknotes hidden away in the barn, and there was talk of a buried churn full of fivers somewhere on the property, though she knew not where. The men of the house were 'untrained to comfort', knowing nothing of weariness, the weariness she felt not bodily, but deep within. She went out to the gate to check if the morning's milk containers had been stacked by the road ready for collection, knowing full well they would have – Horace the cowhand would be in for his breakfast soon. She lingered at the gate, minding the hens scratching in the weeds, and feeling she had forgotten something she needed to say to her son. 'Think of something like it,' her father would have said. Daft apeth. Florrie shook her head. Her Lyme lot were 'funnyosities', she thought, but rather them than the crow-hearted farmer she had lived with all these years. She could now see the milk lorry rumbling up Back Lane from Baggaley's farm. The post van would follow soon, bringing the coroner's report on Fred's death.

She had sat through the short inquest – she knew what to expect. Death by misadventure, in the bloodless language of these things. She thought on his reported last words: 'He done me this time: he meant to have me.' It was like something from a florid film, a Gainsborough melodrama, not that she ever got to the pictures. The local paper had made a meal out of this part of the story. Why had it happened? Because Y's not Z, her father would have said. She remembered her daughter-in-law's nervous laughter when the men came in with the news of the accident. Few tears were shed, and she couldn't summon them now. Only take in the silence over the unfurrowed fields.

The Thursday, the week before last. Fred works in the farmyard as he does every morning. At seven, Ted comes into the yard to receive his orders for the day. Ted asks his father if he would tend the eleven heifers at the riverfield. It was Ted's job routinely, but today he wants to cut tares in another field. Fred, with reluctance, agrees. At eight, Fred goes off to the mustard field. Ted comes back to the yard at ten to see his father. Ted's sister Bess goes to look for him, but can't find him. Ted goes to the corn field in Fallow Lane, but Fred is not there. He then goes to the pasture next to the river where they keep some heifers and a three-year-old Friesian bull. Fred's cycle is leaning against the field gate. Ted enters the field and sees his father lying on the grass in the middle of the field. A heifer with a calf stands near to him. The bull lies on the ground a hundred yards away, swishing away flies with its tasselled tail.

Fred winces and with effort says, 'Get the fork and keep that bull off.' Ted drives the bull to the other side of the field, and it goes placidly. He returns to the prostrate man. Fred has great difficulty speaking: 'He's done me this time. He meant to have me.'

Ted asks, 'Couldn't you stop him with the fork?'

Fred replies, 'No, I will tell you some other time.' Ted knows the bull has a nose ring, but is not wearing a chain. They have had it since it was six months old, and it has always been quiet and not aggressive. His father has shepherded the beast many times, and he knows his father to be one never to take risks, always keeping a fork near the gate to carry into the field. This fork, his keys and matches are scattered over the ten-acre field. They get the injured man to hospital, many ribs fractured, a raw gash on his chest and a bruise like a spreading pool of Fordson oil on his abdomen. He is conscious but unable to say much of what had happened – he can only tell a locum that the bull had knelt on him, its great bulk compressing his barrel chest. He dies at eight thirty in the evening, 'severe shock' the recorded cause.

Fred had bought life assurance a few years before, which would cover the mortgages and the loans, and this would save them from penury. Ted would take over the running of the farm and slowly shut out his mother – they wouldn't speak for the last twenty years of her long life. Fred has no grave marker, no headstone in the churchyard to mark his time, and the whereabouts of his remains are unknown.

In that late summer Florrie felt like a thorn tree on her native coast, gnarled by time, bent against the westerlies, hardened and eternal. In the evening, with the twilight dumpsey and scattered, she unpegged the last of the washing from the line, thinking of home, Hernlee cottage on Pound Road, overlooking the shimmering blue of Lyme Bay and the mariners launching from the Cobb. How as a child she would cling to her mother as she hung out the laundry, feeling the damp comfort of drying sheets against her face. She noticed a thin blood stain on one of Fred's shirts. She will tear it up for rags, good enough for who it's for.

1940

Felt

In the National Gallery in London hangs a lone picture by the Danish post-Impressionist Vilhelm Hammershøi. Entitled *Interior* from 1899, it depicts a woman in black, alone in a panelled room, her back to the viewer, the light muted, fugitive, only the nape of her neck is luminous, as she stands by heavy nineteenth-century furniture, lost in a silent moment. Hammershøi often painted this woman, his wife Ida, in similar rooms and from similar aspects, in the old merchant's house on Strandgade, near the Copenhagen harbour, where they lived. His work is absorbing and enigmatic, the mood he constructs one of subdued beauty and stillness, but also of profound isolation. His paintings of solitary women, restrained interiors and adept handling of light evoke Vermeer, but his pictures are all of their own. Whenever in town I go and look at the London painting, amid the more lauded Cézannes, Monets and Matisses, and its undertones are always unsettling, a sense of pale slanting ghosts.

My late grandmother was long the clan historian, the hoarder of its tales. From time to time in her last years, from the cupboard under the stairs she would produce an old tin box full of ancient photographs, many printed on tinplate. She would sit at the dining table and recall the stories of the people in the pictures, or at least oddments of detail, sifting the prints through her hands and through her long memory like a registrar, or priest – births, marriages, and especially deaths. Many were of Victorian ancestors, most from a well-to-do, urban, southern branch of her family, obscure relations dressed in their finery, standing stiffly in the studios of photographers in Fulham or Putney or Southampton. But there was also an old album covered in cloth embossed with heraldic patterns. Inside its battered, scrappy pages were a few dozen fading images, some familiar, some unknown. The album had belonged to my grandmother's great aunt Kate – Kate Rasmussen, who lived the last forty years of her life in Denmark, and who died during the first winter of the Nazi occupation of Copenhagen, 1940. How the album and a few bits of jewellery and other items had made it back to England at that time is unknown.

The photo album is foxed and stained with age, the string binding frayed, the pictures crudely glued on to the pages, frustratingly obscuring most of the words written on the reverse sides. There are many of Kate and her Danish husband August, she looking rather distracted, half-amused, rarely gazing directly at the lens, and he wearing a jaunty trilby and easy smile, otherwise the very idea of a conventional middle-aged gentleman of the time. In another set, a table is arrayed with their silver wedding anniversary gifts, with two oval portraits of Kate's late parents affixed to a facing panel, their weary expressions hollow-eyed and desolate. And there are many of Kate's English family, generations of pale chary faces in dim backyards, young men and women in uniform during the First World War, old folks on slatted chairs in gardens in the country wearing looks of faint astonishment at how it all came to this.

But among these snapshots and portraits, and those of

family dogs and cats and old houses, are several that jolt. One shows August at a round table with two younger men – the composition brings to mind one of Cézanne's card player paintings – but they are touching finger tips, and are in earnest concentration, evidently holding a séance. Part of the post-1918 Spiritualist movement, a communing with the war dead (Denmark had, however, been neutral in the war), or merely a dubious afternoon diversion? Another is a small shot of a naked African tribe, lined up for the picture like a football team, a classic piece of colonial exotica, but what's it doing here among the family photographs? Elsewhere there are several half-pictures of August as a younger man, the other half having been cut away – a spurned lover of old, or someone else now forgotten or demeaned? Most intriguing perhaps is a postcard from the island of Sprogø. From shortly after the end of the First World War the small island was used to forcibly house pregnant, unmarried women in terrible asylums, something like the infamous Magdalene Laundries of Ireland…

Smallegade 36 b, København F, 1 December 1940

It is getting late. The street is already dark, and the lamplight in this room is dim. I am old, I am unwell, I am tired. I have no children. When I am gone my family here will receive what I have in the world. For my faraway family in England, what I leave behind is my story.

I was born on 27 October 1869 at Kirkby Underwood in the county of Lincoln, the sixth daughter and tenth child of Thomas and Mary Ann Harrison. My education was a few thin years at the village school, enough to be able to read and spell and add up a bill – but it amounts to little now, those years when we would ask mother what there was to eat, and she would always say, 'bread and chew it'. My father had been a shepherd on the Earl of Ancaster's estate, but when he died, I soon went off to work in service, as we all did, us girls, the ones that lived I mean, most of us at big houses in London. At first, it seemed awful far away, and I missed the fields and skies of home, but after a while I made myself buck up, and I got used to it. And I always saw something of my family, those that were near. My sister Sarah and her husband ran a hackney taxi firm in Islington, and sister Annie lived nearby in Finchley, at least till her husband, weighed down with debts, did himself in by putting his head in the gas oven, poor soul, though he was always in Queer Street, that one. My eldest sister Amy lived in Fulham with her house-painter husband, until they went off back to the old county to make a new life away from the Great City.

Life went on its usual run till the day I met August, who had come to my employers' house to make cabinets, that being his stock-in-trade. I had not met a Dane before, in fact no one from beyond our Empire, and he was already considerable in age, a paunch under his waistcoat, which forever had one button unfastened, and his thick moustache was streaked white as was the hair atop his poll. But there was a tenderness to his ways and I liked his manner of speech, stretching out the words, and how, his eyes bright, he talked of the fields and skies of his homeland, which in the way he told it reminded me of mine. I remember he often had the habit of taking out his watch and chain from his waistcoat pocket, though I'm not sure if this was meant to impress me, as he had made the watch himself and he had a small jewellers and watchmakers concern at home, along with his cabinetry business. Everyone said he did seem a solid prospect.

I had never set my cap at him, but when he told me that he held me dear, we decided to make a go of it, though it was a wrench to leave my sisters and their families, as it meant going off to Denmark to live in his house in Copenhagen. We had a simple wedding and my sisters cried when I parted from them, like we did when our uncles had left England to go to America, leaving only the rhyme made out of their names and those of their bairns, a rhyme of remembrance as we never did see them again: 'Matthew, Mark, Luke and John; Bess, Sal and Harry; Bill, Jo and Tom.' August said Denmark wasn't as distant as the wilds of Illinois, but it's true I've seen them all very little since I left the shores of England.

I was full of excitement that first time out on the mail packet over the German Ocean, leaving behind the land that was all I had known. I took to the sea like an old hand, never sick once, not like poor August – many times I would hold his hand and stroke his neck after he'd sent his dinner over the side. I loved the endless grey waves dancing in the watery light, the skirl of the gulls, the wail of the kittiwakes, the feel of the wind on my glowing face and the thrill of our speed through the swells. Soon we were at Helsingor, which August told me was where Shakespeare had set his Hamlet, and then on to the city, to Copenhagen, where we were to live, four decades or more now.

August had his shop and we our little house in Frederiksberg, on a busy street near the zoo, and we were proud to have a respectable address, we worked hard, trade was good, and we did well. I tried hard to learn the Danish language though that was a struggle too, especially as in the first years it often sounded to me like muddled English. Over time I got by, August was patient, and he and I never needed much more than his family around us, though we weren't to be blessed with children of our own...

Our home city suited us – it was more like an old country town at that time, like Lincoln Uphill maybe, and not like big, sooty London. The air was briny and fresh, the streets wide, the houses full of long friendly windows. And the sea, how I loved it, only a mile or two away, the sight of the masts of docked tall ships I could see over the warehouse roofs always making my heart leap. And all week I looked forward to our Sunday outings to the country, which was very like home, the fields low and gently rolling, and threaded with old lanes and small farms, windmills and dikes. August would tell me about the Norsemen in Lincolnshire and how my home village was once a Danish settlement, the name Kirkby meaning 'village with a church' in the old language, so he said. And I would think of rambling over Rippingale Fen when I was a girl with my brothers and sisters, now all thrown about the world, as I was too. How we would lie under the trees in the Bulby orchard, apple blossoms in our hair, or go collecting wildflowers, whose names we knew as well as those of our family – stitchwort, yellow rattle, meadowsweet, wild tansy. Or spend all day catching fish and eels, barefoot in the Old Beck or the Car Dyke – we'd come home with dirty smocks, and mother would tut and say they were 'blacker than Newgate's knocker'...

With dear August, the best times of all were our holidays in the islands, the smaller ones – they filled me with a strange serenity. We would walk the paths and narrow esplanades, his hand in mine as snug as a fly in a sundew, saying very little, and I could see the sea on all sides, and look up to the lighthouses and down the low cliffs, along the airy strand and toward the skyline, and feel something like belonging.

He has been gone ten years now, and since then I have carried on here, the feeling of life waning a little more each day. These days I spend most of the time in this small, dark room. The dressers are stacked with my Royal Copenhagen plates and ships-in-bottles, there are whale oil lamps on the window-sills and pictures and mementoes of August are hanging on the wall. Most of all, I have here my album – the record of my life, all that it is and has been, here on the pages. I hold it on my lap, and fall asleep only to wake to find it arched on its spine on the floor. When I go to bed, I lie awake like a woman in prison, brooding on old times, as sleep won't come. Sometimes despair rises in my throat like a bird in a chimney, but I know it won't be long now...

It is soon the festival of Jul, but the celebrations won't be the same this year. We have unwanted visitors from the south, our German 'protectors'. Everything tastes as bitter as stewed tea. But today I have been at my sewing and knitting, making decorations with Dorit, my young niece. We made some ornaments for the Juletræ, the Christmas tree, out of some scraps of green and red felt. Dorit reminded me that 'Felt' was the Danish word for 'field'.

Some crows are scuffling at the window. The light is too weak...

1983
Maps of the Home Ground

My father ran a small domestic appliance sales and repair service for forty years. When I was growing up, he would often work late into the night in his 'workshop', in reality a small bench tucked in at the far end of his crammed garage. There he would recondition an ancient upright hoover or fit a new drum to a washing machine, its weighty body precariously leaning against the wall as he worked surgically on its tinny innards, the scene lit only by a rigged car lamp. There was a pervading reek of mastics and WD40 and Swarfega. The sill of the oily window and some salvaged industrial shelf units were lined with boxes of screws, haphazardly sorted in old sweet tins. Rows of recycled Richmond sausage boxes, plywood but reinforced with metal struts, were full of hand tools – planes and bradawls, screwdrivers and pliers. Small tea chests, imprinted with faded images of indentured Indian elephants and Lipton's art deco branding, contained motor parts – housings and hoses and armatures. The bench had been his father's before him and epochs of grease lined the soft worn surface; a vice was affixed to the edge, its lead paint peeling; black rubber vacuum-cleaner belts were looped on the limbs of an old oxidising hobbing iron, its use for mending shoes long superseded. And I remember Dad's hands: cracked, callused, rough as glasspaper. It was a grimy world of mystery to me.

Most of his customers were long-held, the sons and daughters of families his father had known before him. His range rarely extended much beyond the county boundary, the radial arm of his operation not longer than forty miles. Most of his work calls were to the near at hand. His knowledge of this territory was deep, his mental maps formed from an early age and accreted slowly over the years. These cognitive maps were multisensory – roads named not numbered, streets lined with trees he'd seen grow up, houses he'd worked in, the cars parked outside, shops he'd known the owners of, food factories and maltings he knew by their smell or engineering works he could recognise from the machinery din, or the sound of its shift siren. If need be, he'd stop often at houses he knew to ask the way. This way he made space into place. He knew equally the old farms lost down narrow tracks in the wolds or the fens, and the pre-war estates of semis built on marginal land near the A1 or the rail lines. He had a story for each one, his method of remembering.

He did have a small collection of folding maps, stuffed into the glove compartment of his estate car or van. They were all from the early 1960s, when he had started out, decorated with colourful adverts for long dead businesses, and showing the vermiculations of old street patterns of the cities of the East Midlands, Nottingham, Leicester, Derby, Peterborough, before their cores were gutted by redevelopment or the green fields on the rims filled with new estates and ring roads. He remained ever hazy about one-way systems and motorways, often relying on slow routes known to his horse-powered forebears, and seared into his memory after fog-cloaked journeys in the coal-fire era, when he could scarce see ahead further than the bonnet of his van. These maps became sources of fascination for me as a young boy, my early geographic training, spending hours under my grandfather's desk re-drawing charts, or composing new ones of imaginary places, island fortresses or continental masses full of familiar topographies. For Dad though, they were rarely used twice, his internal wayfinder seeing him back to the same places time and again.

Dad's place learning had begun early. He had customised his bike, fashioning soft rubber handles from an old inner tube, and he had explored the home town with his best friend Ian, often getting into boyhood scrapes retold many times later. Scrumping apples from an orchard on Halls Hill was a favourite pastime – 'I don't know why', he'll say, 'I don't even like apples. We did it just for the devilment.' Inevitably perhaps they were eventually rumbled by the owner, ruefully taking their reprimand while their friend Rod sat silent and unnoticed in the branches above. Ian was always the source of some scheme or other. He kept a stash of forbidden cigarettes inside the bench seat of a disused milk dray at the old dairy, where they would furtively smoke until rain seeped in and turned the fags into a soggy heap. Or else he'd use a short metal ruler, routinely kept in his top pocket, to insert into slot machines dispensing chewing gum. Often, he would play with fire – Dad would never forget when Ian dropped his Webley air pistol, shooting a pellet into his cheek just under the eye… The two boys roamed widely over their locale, imprinting its contours, grading the camber of their roads, maximising their homegrown fun.

Boundaries dissolved and reformed with each new day. As a young clerk, Dad would deliver company bills and mail by bike to save on stamps – and then got the company to pay for derailleur gears. Sometimes he'd be sent for mythical items at phantom places, for an office lark – to buy a ball of Whitworth thread (the helix of a screw) at Ponton Docks (a damp village near the confluence of two rivers) or a jar of elbow grease at Upton Vinegar Mills (long since torn down). At the same time, Dad was developing his abiding passion for motor vehicles, adding new layers to his knowledge of the country. He learned to drive before his teens, famously backing up a 10-ton lorry down a narrow driveway when helping his father on a Saturday morning delivery. He would grasp any opportunity to take the wheel. When he was still only fifteen, he delivered a car sold in the Saturday market, steering while the car was pulled by horse and cart down the main road. Days after his seventeenth birthday, he passed his driving test and he would then borrow his father's Vauxhall 10 to take his friends around the village pubs. After writing it off on the narrow bends near Burton Coggles, he bought his own car, a Ford Anglia, and weekends from then on would see a diligent regimen of cleaning and maintenance. After he had met my mother, he would rise early in the morning and drive the fifteen-mile round trip to the farm and then to town to take her to work, before returning home for breakfast. Once married, he would take his new father-in-law out for Sunday drives, never going further than ten miles from the farm, but all unknown regions to the older man. All the while Dad was adding to his mastery of the district. Where his ancestors had known all about horses, he knew engines.

In the early 1980s Dad worked long hours, struggling in a hard economy. A short man in his early forties, though looking much younger, in winter he would be wrapped in multiple coats against the bone-chilling cold in the unheated garage. The winters of those years saw great snowstorms and ice would lock tight the doors of his van, needing boiled kettles to loosen them. Often between Christmas and New

Year he would be required to mend washing machines and irons, against an archaic superstition of having no dirty laundry in the house as the year turned. In the small terraced houses in town, there would often be little room for a twin-tub washer, but Dad, enterprising as ever, sold them to double as hallway tables, covered with a tablecloth and handy for siting the telephone.

After long stints in the garage and nearing pub closing time, Ian would sometimes call from the path on his way for a last-orders pint. Dad would call it a day, wash his hands in an icy bucket and go 'up the road' with him. Their connection was long, mostly unvoiced but always present. They had first met at Mablethorpe beach as six-year-olds in 1948 on the works week away, Ian's father a butcher, Dad's a grocer. They had travelled there by taxi, fifty-odd miles, as few had cars in the post-war years, and the taxi had punctures on the way, thin austerity tyre rubber pierced by the horseshoe nails that still littered the road at that time, vestige of the animal cartage now at the end of its day. Luggage had fallen off the roof rack somewhere between Dogdyke and Tattershall Castle – the roads still had no signposts, having been taken down during the invasion threat of 1940 – and they had had to go back some miles, to find it lying undisturbed in the middle of the road like an abandoned hoard. They had loved the seaside, the wavering breath of air under the summer sun, the new grounds to discover, the donkey rides on the beach, pleasures to be had free and gratis. Dad's father had been stricken with a cold, but hated any fuss, any 'splotheram' in the Nordic Lincolnshire dialect. Instead, refusing to be 'badly', he'd dip his cigarette in Penetrol cold remedy, a foul, tarry decongestant, and beat a raw egg into a mug of milk, down it in one gulp and reckon he was then right as rain. These founding myths are still rolled out when Dad and Ian get together, seventy years on, the constructed pillars of a long friendship.

Whenever we now visit my parents, in the old county, my wife and I can still ask Dad the route for a day out with our children. The answer will be long and involved, but always garlanded with old tales and precise information not to be gleaned from a satnav. His mental maps have become his source of nested memory of the world, his knowing of the home ground through storytelling, the assurance that he won't lose his way.

1990

Waiting for the Sun

It is December 1990, I have just turned twenty-one, and I am far from home. As I cross the main square and into the long street, I see the stooping figure of my Flemish friend Han standing outside the Café Metamorphose across from the International Student House. We are exchange students in the city of Groningen in the agricultural far northeast of the Netherlands, a half hour from the Ems estuary and the German border, and not here to learn farming. Han is framed by the door, braided light from a transom window arching over his tight-curled hair. He is a little ashen-faced but bearing up well after the heavy night before of whisky and *roken*. He is leaning slightly into the midwinter wind blustering down Oude Boteringestraat. Older than me, by a month, he has a European sophistication I can only imbibe in arthouse movies in the Student Kinema down the road. He has a rolled cigarette of Dutch Zware shag tobacco between his fingers, wafting smoke as he cups his hand to guard the lit end. He'll not burn a hole in his cashmere scarf.

Han makes to say something, then just raises a hand, and fixed in silence, mouths a self-directed '*ja*' and gives a slight nod. I have been seeing Francesca, a girl from the South, from Padua, turn right at Venice. Dark, ardent and striking, she has made me forget myself. In my self-mythology, I am lost in a movie, *Saturday Night and Sunday Morning* remade by Kieslowski. But now her sick boyfriend from home has arrived, fragile, scarred, needing her. The thought of this lays on my mind like grit.

I first came to the House with an English friend and fellow student in the late summer, a hot August sun gilding its redbrick facade and glinting off its picture windows. For me, in the months since, it has become part sanctuary and part madhouse. Formerly housing the Psychology department, the House has been hastily repurposed by the University as jury-rigged accommodation for foreign students on short study programmes. The walls of its narrow rooms are white woodchip, the floor a thin veneer, the windows won't open, and red warning lights still hang outside the doors, legacy of past research trials and consultations. It's like living in a filing-cabinet. Some Saturdays afternoons I curl up in my nest here, reading old novels and ignoring course books, or listening to the English football scores on the BBC World Service, the incantation of familiar team names now sounding far-flung. Sometimes I fall asleep in the late afternoon and wake in the grey light of morning with pigeons scuffing on the ledge outside, one of the vast sleeps of these years that seem to cross continents.

Two Dutch postgraduates in their early twenties, the debonair Jan-Pieter and jolly Jan-Jaap, are nominally in charge of the House, and indeed they are always good for recommendations of beerhalls and coffeeshops and from where to 'borrow' bikes. Otherwise, there are thirty or so young people, mostly from Europe, with small groups of Indians and Africans and Americans. My great friend Han is one of a number of Belgians, far enough from home to allow licence and reinvention, but comfortable with the language and culture. French, Spanish and Germans mix with Eastern Europeans, newly able to travel abroad and not yet used to Western plenitude. Coming home late from the pub, I often see a small group of friendly Slovaks, huddled in the kitchen, cooking vast pots of midnight rice with brown sugar, aprons over their thin brown sweaters. A solitary, older Russian seems as lonely as a Van Gogh chair, and is seen only rarely out of the shadows – but perhaps he keeps more sensible hours than I do. There are two communal places, where we gather in the evenings: first, the large kitchen with long refectory tables and multiple ovens, sofas near a small TV and a single, much-used telephone point. Second, is a laundry room, strung with drying lines and, incongruously, two full-size table tennis tables – epics of ping-pong are played here, especially after nights out, usually hare-brained multinational doubles games, the air thick with exhortations and curses in miscellaneous tongues as we slither barefoot over the damp wooden floor.

Later, home again in England, the House will seem to me something of a lost domain. The kitchen is a perfumed place of exotic foods, cooked and consumed with ceremony and love. If there is a party coming up, in a bright corner there will be stacked bottles of wine, jenever and Dutch lager, ready for the taking. Interior clouds of blue-grey cigarette smoke drift among the ceaseless chatter in international English, fortunately for me the lingua franca. A corkboard is pinned with postcards from roaming inmates, insider jokes scrawled on the back, and photographs of house dinners, or the feast of Sinterklaas, Jan-Jaap dressed up as a convincing St Nicholas. I know all the faces now as well as I know those of my village back home. I am anchored amid the shouts of excited laughter, the earnest discussions of a generation, the feathery traces of sex, the ache of longings of young people away from home. I am entranced.

Francesca enters this scene later, arriving in the autumn with her amiable, sad-eyed friend Simone. They invite me to eat with them, my first real Italian dinner, polenta, risotto, flavourful salads, which I wolf while drinking too much red wine. She is immediately so open, direct and tactile, which I am unused to, and we spend hours talking in the kitchen, of all things, light and dark. I feel the warm attentiveness of her green eyes upon me, as we take long night walks through the city, and she tells me her long-time boyfriend in Italy is now of the past. We play pool in dive bars, sit restlessly in underlit jazz clubs and share glasses of iced water in hot dance halls, emerging late into light-spangled streets, clasping each other against the cold. A week later she tells me she wants to cut my long hayrick hair to see better my eyes, now wide open and expectant. She sits me down in the female toilets, and I smile into her sultry face as she snips away the fringe, spindling curls round her forefinger. In her most velvet voice she says she feels she met me a long time ago. Committed to her scientific studies, she spends long hours at the lab where I sometimes bring her coffee as if bearing an elixir, and we steal kisses over the periodic table. She leaves me notes on scraps of printed molecular diagrams – 'you are my man now – Definitely!' She is puckish, bright-eyed, feline; her features are strong, her mouth sardonic, her touch tender. It seems inevitable that I will fall for her. Nights with her dissolve into day, years might roll by, I awake in her arms feeling I am the subject of a benediction. My friends aren't too sure of this new entanglement, mistrustful of motives, but I am locked in her holding pattern, deep in the drama of our intimacy.

Han and I hold a joint twenty-first birthday party in the kitchen. Jan-Pieter has rigged a sound system, and Han plays his Doors records, our fires truly lit. Francesca's ill boyfriend arrives the same day, and she and I can only give each other knowing sidelong glances. I can't bring myself to dislike him; short and fair like me, his nervous sadness could have been mine. He smokes incessantly, deploying a kind of grim circular breathing technique in order to chain cigarettes. When he speaks his voice cracks from a harrowed throat. I spend much of the party speaking to Kathy, a tall arts postgrad from New York who acted as our student 'mentor' when we first arrived in Holland. We like each other, and I notice, not unaware of the irony, that Francesca stares with jealousy at our close conversation. The night ends with renditions of 'Happy Birthday', Han and I grinning unsteadily, full of drink and dangerous confusion. I don't expect the tears that come to my eyes; I stifle them.

In the morning I need to escape the heady atmosphere of this place. As of old, I want to be in the open air, to ease my anxious state. I am resolved to walk and to keep walking. I wave to Han and turn the corner, passing the Academy Tower and its trailing carillon and, in the way I think at twenty-one, say goodbye to that part of my life for, well, a few hours anyway. Holland is a benign country for the walker, though this December the air is glassy with cold and everywhere there is water. As a geography student, this is the stuff of field trips, when I can get up for them on time: a nation heaved from the waves. Hunched in their small cars, our professors have driven me and other foreign students right across the country, personal tours of the great continental flood-prone rivers of the Maas, Rhine and Scheldt that drain into the sea here, their silty debris forming the original hinterlands. Our teachers show us how after ten centuries of beavering the country has been scaffolded on sluices, dykes and dams. Beside the enclosed Zuider Zee we have half an hour standing quivering with cold on the twenty-mile boulder clay limb of the Afsluitdijk, the eel-fishing lake IJsselmeer behind it. A few miles further, we visit the Delta Works scheme that shortens the coast, a huge buffer against surging North Sea storms. Everywhere you go in Holland it's the grand Dutch attempt at dominion over water. In Groningen, canals and moats form concentric rings round the old city and I now make for the first of them.

The rain is siling down as I cross the Grote Markt, past remnant gabled houses and the Martinitoren, whose bells are said still to have bullet holes from the Battle of Groningen in the last weeks of the Second World War. Many nights the marketplace has been my square of choice for a late-night visit to FEBO, *De Lekkerste*, 'the tastiest', frites with mayo, perfect soak-up after six bottles of Grolsch at the back-alley Het Pakhuis pub. Today, I keep going, rain now and then dribbling off the back of my Dutch bargeman's cap that I think makes me look like Dylan circa '61, and riveleting down under my collar with delicious misery. Into the radial roads, I go beyond the sad red-light district, the pool bars and coffeeshops and brown cafes and, then expected and unexpected at the same time, neat storefronts selling cheeses, colossal Goudas and Edams plattered in the window. Further on, and over the bridge, staring into the rainfed canal, I see only my pallid face reflected back.

I get to the Noorderplantsoen, the North Park, more pond than park. Some weeks before it was the scene of a fabled international football game, all of us playing like charmed actors, all deft touches and visionary runs, lofted passes and low-rifled volleys. This contest of *totaalvoetbal* ended after I toe-ended a shot over the 'bar' and into the serpentine, sending black swans gusting into the air – we spent a long time trying to coax the ball back but eventually someone cracked open some beers and Lucky Strikes and we sloped off into the grey afternoon, sweaters tied round our midriffs.

Now the park is deserted. I walk across looking for a war memorial – a British lecturer at the university has told us of the role of the Noorderplantsoen in the Battle of Groningen forty-five years before. The Canadians fought their way through the park after days of heavy fire, the other entry points to the city having been destroyed by the retreating German troops. Little Stalingrad, they called this desperate late siege. I think of the German students in the Student House, even now skirting and apologetic though it was all nothing to do with them. I think of my grandfathers, grateful they had been non-combatants.

I leave the park, and looking for the river, turn west, and as I cross the road see two friends from the Student House filling up their car with petrol. David and Mila are Catalan dramatists and actors, in Holland to study some aspect of northern theatre. They are in their mid-thirties and thus vastly old in my eyes. They speak almost no English and the limit of my Spanish has been to tell them once *soy iglesias* ('I'm a church') instead of *soy ingles* ('I'm English'). But, in the spirit of that house, we communicate well enough, especially over beer and in a haze of smoke. I gather now that they are on a day trip to the coast and hoping to catch the ferry out to the Wadden Islands. I hadn't figured on company today but their affecting entreaties, all dark smiles and furrowed brows – they know why I am drifting around alone – soon have me wedged in the back of the tiny VW and thankful, out of the driving rain.

We are soon in the unsoiled blandness of the edge of town, past the growing Paddepoel university complex, where I should be, hunkered down in the library with tabulated statistics on the Randstad. We take a minor road, following the course of the Reitdiep, the canalized old River Hunze, now in sections drainpipe-straight, the stuff a geometrist's dreams are made on. How much of a memory of its former fluvial ways does it retain? There are no river craft, no anglers under umbrellas, no people at all. Few trees line its banks, apart from odd sentinel alders, drooped against the boundless backcloth of dark skyforms. Variegated and heaped cumuliform clouds slowly smear into low banks of rain-filled stratus as if blotched by hand. A few drenched rooks are assembling in the fields. I see a lone song-thrush, hammering snail-shells on a stone. The car's overworked heater takes an edge off the cold, but I shiver behind still upturned lapels.

The wide plain of agricultural land opens out. It was traditionally poor and communist in Groningen province – a statue of Lenin adorned the main square in the village of Tjuchem – and the scene of angry land battles earlier in the century. The farmers here are well known for their fatalism and melancholy – I met a farmer's daughter in a bar and she told me the stock response to a how-are-you on the polders was 'Could be worse'. I know the same kind of transcending pessimism back home in the fields on the Lincoln Edge. The soil mirrors the sky, black and slick as a crow's back.

As it did when I was a child, long car travel settles my mind. I sit back, leaning my head on the rubbery seals of the window, watching the rinsing of the windscreen and the sodden contourless landscape of winter crops. The whirr of the wipers lulls me into half-sleep. Whispery threads of a conversation I can't understand percolate from the front.

We pass through small neat villages, Dorkwerd, Oostum, Garnwerd, each with storybook windmills and redbrick churches at their centre that seem fleetingly to redden the rain. Near Aduarderzijl, we veer west, and the river becomes meandering again, momentarily unconstrained. We find the main road and head towards Friesland, a land of poets and dreamers according to our professor. We pass through *terp* villages, built on mounds in the Middle Ages as islands in the flood. As we enter the Marne region, the sky lightens a little, and the wind rises. We can sense the sea, past the reedy network of inland waterways and amphibious army testing grounds. When we had been here the week before on a field trip, these channels had been sleety and iced over, skaters in scarves making the scene for a moment resemble a medieval book of hours handmade by Breughel. We skirt the Lauwersmeer, another of those encapsulated former seas, and its flocks of late-leaving, slender-limbed waders on the saltings. Soon after, we come into Lauwersoog, the ferry port for the islands, once reputedly a Roman trading post, now a concrete harbour town.

As the ferry eases out of the harbour into the Waddenzee, I go up on deck, gripping the rimy handrail but glad to be outside again, deep in the pocket of winter. The rain has stopped. I watch a skein of overwintering wild geese, closely following their patterns of flight. I think of the film we'd been to see last week, *Citizen Kane*, a classic. I loved one scene above all: an old man recalls a ferry crossing many years before when he sees a girl in a white dress with a white parasol, seeing her only for a second, but thereafter never forgotten. Francesca had laughed at me of course, my romantic dolour.

The sea is now a mass of hefty rolling waves lashed white by the winds, but after a while the foreshore of the island appears ahead low and languorous, its long slumped phocine form extending towards the easterly sandbars. Schiermonnikoog, the 'island of the grey monks', a small bone in the long fossil back of the archipelago. During the summer, my Dutch friends go on *wadlopen* tours, walking to the island over the mudflats at low tide, a strange half-world, unveiled twice a day like a sludgy Atlantis. Crossing tidal gullies and steering clear of the deeper channels, eyes always on the weather and the shifting sandbanks, they spot seals and wading birds. Small yachts loop through the shoals, like something out of *The Riddle of the Sands*, Erskine Childers' Edwardian spy thriller set in the Frisian islands a few miles east of here.

The island's red lighthouse comes into view, and I go off to find David and Mila. Disembarking among the few visitors, outnumbered by storm-buffeted birds, I immediately feel freedom. The wide dunes stretch east and west, with only some hardy day-trippers beachcombing, holding flapping maps. The island's village is a cluster of old houses built perpendicular to the prevailing winds. The cold is urgent here, consuming every mote of warmth, but leaving us shining. We go into a hotel bar. A cat is sleeping by a great friendly fire, and we stand at the bar, and among a bloom of choices, have coffee and brandy. Our few words don't matter – we use them over and over in delight. Stepping outside, we walk along cycle paths and the strand, tasting spindrift. Marram grass and fescues are colonising the foredunes, tough binders used by wild rabbits for cover. Beyond the beach cusp, onto the littoral, a small flock of oystercatchers forage for bivalves, stealing in between the swash and backwash of breaking waves. A larger group of lapwings probe the mudflats, then in tottering flight launch into the wind. They have always been my favourite birds, gleaming green, black and white on the ploughed field at the back of my childhood home. The watery low-angled sun makes me squint along the shoreline. It is time to leave.

It is a cellar-dark night by the time we reach the House. Han is in the hall with his bike, looking much less etiolated than the morning. We walk along the corridor swapping news of the day. The door of the strip-lit kitchen is open, throwing a synthetic light on the bottom of the stairwell. I look up to see Francesca disappearing to the first floor with the boyfriend behind her.

Months later, but while I still have a keen appetite for self-deception, she sends me a postcard. The scene is generic, a sunrise over a shimmering river. On the back she has written 'Waiting for the sun'. It takes me a while to track down the old Doors lyrics: 'We race down to the sea/ Standing there on Freedom's shore/ waiting for the sun … waiting for you to hear my song/ waiting for you to come along …' I feel like I am swimming in an underground river that never emerges.

I do see her again. The next New Year holidays, she invites me to a freezing refuge high in the Italian Alps along with twenty of her Paduan friends, including, unbeknownst to me, her new boyfriend. I grew up at sea level, and in the high elevation I just get drunk and altitude sickness. Later, she sends me another card: *Spero che la prossima montagna da scalare ti renda solamente felice* – 'I hope the next mountain you climb will only make you happy.'

My wife likes to hear this story; we sometimes compare what we were like in our twenties, our unhappinesses, our frosted dreams, long before we met. We live in sunny uplands now, overlooking the sea, and far from the waters of the low countries.

Mum and her father, North End Farm, 1950s

Acknowledgements

A version of '1963: Dreams of the Old West' first appeared online at Caught by the River.

My thanks to:

Adrian, Gracie, Graham and Jon at Little Toller Books.

Friendly readers Ziyad Marar, the late Nick Bellorini, Paul Machin, Craig Smith, Roy McMillan, Han Fraeters, Huw Alexander, Jeff Barrett, John Andrews, Evelyn Dunwoody.

My parents, Janet and Robin Sentance.

Above all, Kate, Evie and Noah.

Published by Little Toller Books in 2019

Text © Neil Sentance 2019

The right of Neil Sentance to be identified as the author of this work has been asserted by him in accordance with Copyright, Design and Patents Act 1988

Photography © Neil Sentance 2019

Typeset in Garamond by Little Toller Books

Printed in India by Imprint Press

All papers used by Little Toller Books are natural, recyclable products made from wood grown in sustainable, well-managed forests

A catalogue record for this book is available from the British Library

ISBN 978-1-908213-65-5